Tube Walks:
Countryside Walks from London's Underground Stations

Tube Walks:
Countryside Walks from London's Underground Stations

Nicholas Taylor

First Edition 2016

Copyright © 2016 by Nicholas Taylor

All rights reserved. This book or any portion thereof may not be reproduced or used in any manner whatsoever without the express written permission of the publisher except for the use of brief quotations in a book review or scholarly journal.

Maps © OpenSteetMap contributors.
Contains Ordnance Survey data © Crown copyright and database right 2010-12
Maps used under data available under the Open Database License CC BY-SA.
For further information: http://www.openstreetmap.org/copyright

First Printing: 2016

ISBN 978-1-326-81725-1

Contents

Acknowledgements 6
Introduction 7
High Barnet to Finchley Central 10
Mile End to Angel 17
Epping to Loughton 20
Morden to Putney Bridge 26
Cockfosters Circular 32
Rickmansworth to Uxbridge.. 37
Tottenham Hale to Stratford....................................... 43
Westbourne Park to King's Cross 48
Richmond to Southfields... 51
Oakwood to Arnos Grove... 59
Highgate to Finsbury Park 62
Woolwich Arsenal Circular... 66
Further Walking 72
Note 73

Acknowledgements

Thanks must go to everyone who walked with me while researching this book and the walks. Thanks especially to Mum who washed all my dirty trousers! Thanks also have to go to people who suggested walks and locations and to all those invaluable people in the Twitter-sphere.

Thanks also to Open Street Maps and their users and contributors for their use of the maps in this book. I've only included maps where absolutely necessary to aid you navigation.

Introduction

Walking has been one of Britain's great pastimes. Since the Kinder Trespass in 1932, the British walker has been able to ramble right across the country. The Countryside and Rights of Way Act 2000 established the right to roam across the hills and moors and many other areas of our countryside. Public rights of way exist across the country, allowing people the freedom to walk, and it's quite common to see large groups, couples and individuals roaming the land.

For those of us living in London and passionate about the outdoors, it can be hard to find time to get out and enjoy the countryside. Finding routes, booking trains and planning accommodation all take precious time away from the walk. The walks in this book have been designed with the London walker in mind. By using Underground and DLR stations as start and end points it is hoped that you will be able to explore the quieter parts of the city without great expense and without the hassle of long journeys, finding parking and booking campsites. The walks in this book are of various lengths, most are perfect for a morning or an afternoon walk. All walks can be completed alone, with canine company or with family and friends.

All have been carefully researched and planned, however things on the ground do change. You should always be prepared for diversions to footpaths, particularly on more urban walks. As London expands, construction and redevelopment works take place often, and often force local diversions. Therefore, I recommend the OS Explorer Maps (161, 162, 173, 174) or an A-Z style map should get you out of a tricky spot. If you find a permanent change, please do let me know for future editions. Use of a compass and advanced navigation techniques will not be required, so these walks are ideal for those starting out.

While walking, it is always best to carry a few basic supplies. Waterproofs are a good idea, even in summer! Most paths are fairly well made and don't require technical walking boots, but good comfortable shoes are always recommended and should avoid blisters. I've included details about the path surface so you can be prepared before you set out. A simple first aid kit is also worth carrying, as is a bottle of water.

When walking, the principle of 'take only memories, leave only footprints' is very important. If you stop for lunch, make sure you take all rubbish away with you. Be especially careful not to disturb any of the precious wildlife you may encounter. Although we're not in the wilds, it's worth reminding yourself of the countryside code.

Finally, remember walking should be fun. Whether you walk for fitness, to observe nature, or simply because you enjoy putting one foot in front of the other, make sure you keep getting outside and enjoying the great outdoors.

High Barnet to Finchley Central

| High Barnet | Northern Line | Zone 5 |
| Finchley Central | Northern Line | Zone 4 |

Approx. 4.5 miles   2 hours

A quiet brook from London's heights. Walking mostly on well-made paths and gravel tracks.

The people of High Barnet, it seems, are very keen on pointing out the height of the town. Local lore says that the town is the highest point until you reach the Ural Mountain Range. Also on the theme of height, the imposing parish church has a plank of wood in its tower reportedly to show the same height as the dome of St. Paul's Cathedral. The tower is open on Saturdays throughout the summer and is well worth a visit if you can, it is a short walk uphill from the start of the walk.

This walk follows the Dollis Brook Trail. The Brook flows into the River Brent, which in turn flows into the River Thames. The Dollis Brook Greenwalk, as it is often referred to, begins in Moat Mount Open Space, in Mill Hill, and runs for 10 miles to Hampstead Heath. The Greenwalk can be used as a link between London's two orbital paths, the London LOOP and the Capital Ring. The Greenwalk is waymarked with green disks showing a white arrow.

There are many open spaces along the route, as well as local nature reserves. Many plants grow along the banks of the brook and this encourages wildlife too. Kingfishers and Moorhens have been spotted along the brook.

High Barnet station, the end of this branch of the Northern Line, opened in 1872 and is on the original site of the, now famous, Barnet Fair. Originally used to trade horses from the North, it has since given its name for cockney rhyming slang for 'hair'.

Leave the station by the lower exit, climbing to the main road then head down the hill. On a good day, the view across the city is excellent. You can also look down on the old Underhill Stadium, where Barnet F.C. used to play home matches. A Barnet oddity was to have a sloping pitch, meaning one team would always be playing uphill! At the time of writing, there are controversial plans to turn the stadium into a school. Continue down the main road (A1000).

At the railway bridge, turn right onto Fairfield Way, which becomes Grasvenor Avenue. At the end of the road you will find a tarmac path that follows the route of the Dollis Brook. Watch out for cyclists also using the path. You will pass through Brook Farm Open Space which was used in the 18th Century to grow hay, feeding London's growing horse population. Keep heading south until you reach a main road beside Totteridge and Whetstone station.

Turn right and head downhill, following the main road. Cross the road at the opening to the next section of the Dollis Brook walk. Again, this section is open to cyclists as well as walkers. The walk continues following the brook on a slightly more enclosed section of the path. This is a very popular route for local dog walkers. At the gate, cross Laurel Road and continue following the brook. At the next gate, look out for a signpost turning you right along Tillingham Way. At the end of the road turn left onto Southover Way. There is a small green arrow on a lamppost to remind you. Continue past the houses for about 250 metres and lookout on the left for the gates and signpost for the Dollis Brook Greenwalk. Continue on the tarmac path to Argyle Road (see map).

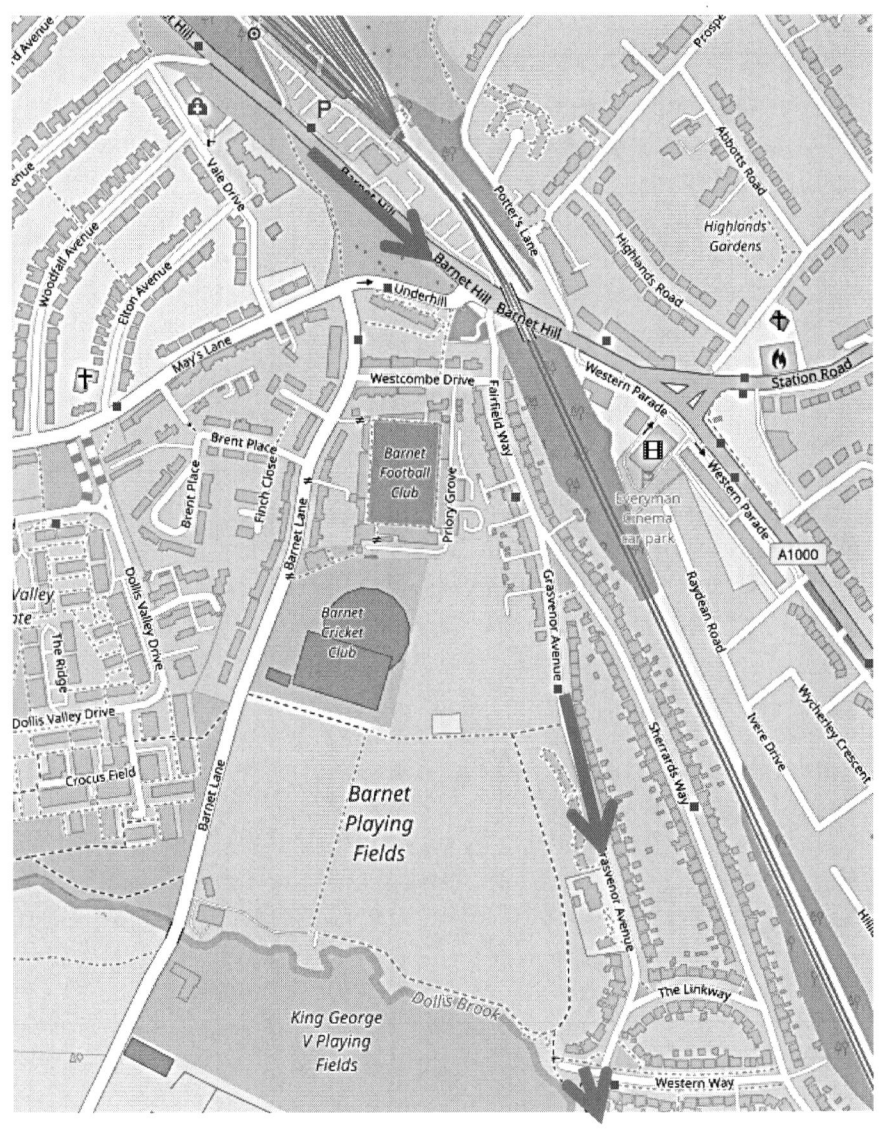

Cross the road. The path, still tarmac, winds its way past a children's play park. A slight right at the next road, Firsby Avenue, to continue following the Greenwalk through the local allotments. You will then be into a more wooded section alongside Finchley Golf Course. After the allotments cross the bridge and take the small gravel path on the bank of the brook. When you emerge at the next bridge, continue in the same direction on the tarmac path. Cross the wooden bridge over the brook and continue along the tarmac. At the fork, bear right to the signpost then turn right. Cross the bridge. You may begin to hear the rumble of the trains going over the viaduct.

At the end of the path, you will emerge onto Dollis Road. Look right and you will see another of Barnet's heights. The Dollis Brook viaduct, built in 1867, now carries Northern Line trains between Mill Hill East and Finchley Central. The viaduct is the highest point above ground level anywhere on the London Underground Network (although it isn't the highest point on the network).

To get to Finchley Central station, turn left along Dollis Road and at the mini roundabout, turn right onto Nether Street. The station is at the top of the hill. If you are feeling more adventurous, the Dollis Brook Greenwalk continues to Hampstead Heath where it links up with the Capital Ring. The path is marked on the OS Explorer Map. Another extension would be to follow the viaducts path towards Mill Hill East. There is a section of planned line beyond the station that is accessible from Sanders Lane. Note, however, that trains from Mill Hill East are less frequent than on the rest of the line.

Further information on the Dollis Brook Greenwalk can be obtained from Barnet Council who have produced an excellent leaflet and guide to the whole 10 mile walk. Information boards also provide excellent information at points of interest.

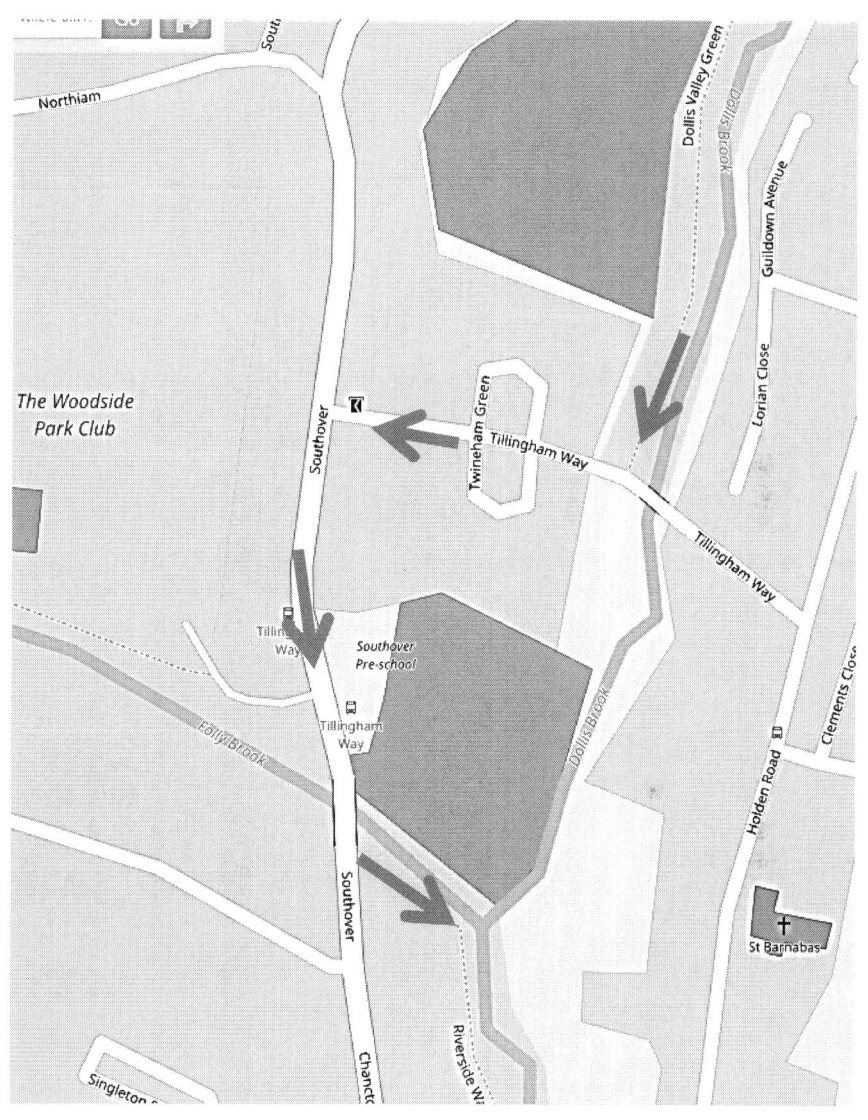

Mile End to Angel

Mile End   Central, District and
                  Hammersmith & City Lines   Zone 2

Angel   Northern Line   Zone 1

                  Approx. 4 miles   1 ½ hours

The once busy commercial canal now provides a ribbon of peace through noisy North London.

This pleasant walk follows the Regent's Canal towpath so navigation is very easy! As you walk, you will find examples of the canal's previous industrial use, with many of the warehouses now converted to homes and studios. The hustle and bustle of the canal's previous industrial use has now been replaced by that of its new recreational users. There are plenty of canal side pubs, bars and cafes too. The path is very popular with walkers, dog walkers, joggers as well as cyclists.

This wasn't always the case however. As industrial traffic on the canal moved to railways and lorries, the canal fell into disrepair. Luckily, however, a new use was found for the canal. The original idea to turn the canal into a railway was shelved; instead electrical cables are housed under the towpath, cooled by the water from the canal. These cables now form part of the National Grid. The canal is also very important for London's Wildlife. Moorhens, mallards and swans can be found using the canal and there are some fish too, although you need to look hard to find them! The canal is used extensively by pleasure craft, kayak and canoeists, and there are plenty of colourful house boats moored alongside the path.

Leave Mile End station and turn left along Mile End Road. Ahead, you will notice the Green Bridge, an extension of Mile End Park. The park is famous as the site where 60,000 Men of Essex camped and met Richard II during the 1381 Peasants' Revolt. Climb the steps onto the bridge, and look left to see Canary Wharf standing tall. Turn right on the bridge and follow the path as it winds its way down to the canal. As you reach the canal, turn right and take the towpath alongside the water. The path can be busy with cyclists, so please look and listen out.

Pass the Mile End Park Arts Pavilion on your right and continue alongside the canal. Look out for the birdlife using the canal for home and food. As you continue, you will pass a viewing platform that forms part of the Mile End Park Ecology Pavilion. Continue past the sculptures and over the bridge. This bridge marks the end of the Hertford Union Canal, a short canal that links the Regent's Canal and the River Lee Navigation. Continue towards Old Ford Lock. The cottage and stables are Grade 2 Listed Buildings.

As you pass the lock, you will now be alongside Victoria Park. The park, which opened in 1845, has many unique features, including surviving alcoves of the original London Bridge and a Chinese Pagoda that was originally installed in Hyde Park for a Chinese Exhibit. You will see the pagoda as you pass on the towpath. Victoria Park also has free to use public toilets, two cafes and a boating lake. Continue along the canal and pass by the large entrance to Victoria Park.

Continue to the next lock, Acton's Lock. Here the cottages look more tired. On the opposite bank, you will see Laburnum Boat Club, which often has groups of youngsters out in kayaks and canoes. Carry on along the towpath to Sturt's Lock where you will find a signpost pointing you to Angel Station. Ignore the turn off the towpath to the right and continue along the canal. After two basins on your left and City Road lock, you will come to the Islington Tunnel. As there is no towpath, barges used to be legged through, until the installation of a steam tug which used a chain on the canal bed to heave barges through the tunnel.

At the tunnel entrance, turn right and take the steep path up to street level. Cross at the zebra crossing and continue in the same direction along Duncan Street. At the end, turn left onto the main road (A1) and finish the walk at the station. The route can be continued, if you wish, to the vibrant and busy Camden. Follow the waymarks in the pavement to continue the walk on the west side of the tunnel.

More information on the canals can be found from the Canal and River Trust website.

Epping to Loughton

| Epping | Central Line | Zone 6 |
| Loughton | Central Line | Zone 6 |

Approx. 5½ miles   2 hours

A walk through the historic woodland, mostly on gravel tracks, but some parts on muddy, woodland paths. Includes some steep climbs and descents.

This walk takes you through the historic Epping Forest. The whole forest is over 6000 acres and is around 12 miles long, although is only 2½ miles wide at its widest point. It is thought that it gained Royal Forest status in the 12th Century. Granted by Henry 2nd, the Royal Forest status meant that only the king could hunt there, which is the historical meaning for the word forest. Although only the king could hunt, commoners were allowed to graze their animals and forage food and wood from the forest. In 1878, the Epping Forest Act gave care of the forest to the City of London Corporation and the act also stopped the forest from being enclosed and built on.

The forest is a Site of Special Scientific Interest (SSSI) and a wide variety of species can be found. Numerous trees support a wealth of invertebrates and, hidden among the branches, you may spot fallow deer, muntjac or even an adder. Now the forest is enjoyed by many people and can be particularly busy on a sunny weekend. Keep an eye out for mountain bikers and horse riders as you explore this ancient forest.

The walk begins at Epping Station, the very last on the Central line. It is about 40 minutes from central London and can be quite bouncy at the end of the line! The station has the largest car park on the network, supporting the many people from surrounding towns who commute into London. The station is also the start/end point for the Essex Way, a long distance footpath to Harwich Old Lighthouse.

Leave the station, turn right and head up the road. Look out for a small path, fenced, on the left. Follow the path around the car park and up the steps to the road. Turn left and follow the road. Turn right onto Western Avenue. Turn right and follow the bridleway. Ignore paths to the left and right and follow the bridleway to an open field. Head towards the bench, bearing slightly right.

Cross the tarmac path to the waymark post and gravel drive. Follow the gravel drive and it becomes a tarmac road. This is the hamlet of Bell Common, where the M25 disappears into a tunnel. Ignore the footpath to the left. Keep following the road to the Forest Gate Inn. Turn left and follow the road, ignoring the bridleway on the left.

After Ivy Chimneys Road, at the three wooden posts, turn right crossing the road and follow the grass path. The path turns left before the cricket ground and passes through woods. Stick to the wide gravel path. Pass the green arrow and follow the path up and down the hill. Pass another green arrow on your left. At the crossing of paths, at the top of the hill, follow the green arrows, sticking to the gravel path.

On the right, you will pass by Ambresbury Banks. There is an information board here, telling you about its history. It is thought it was built sometime around 700-500BC and used until around 42AD. Local legend suggests this was the site of Boudica's death, although this is disputed and there is no evidence of this. The banks are a scheduled monument, as is

Loughton Camp, which you will pass by later. You don't get as good a view however, so take some time to explore the Banks.

Head back to the gravel path. Pass another arrow and ignore paths on the left and right. Carry on to the car park. Cross the road, carefully, to the smaller car park opposite. Bear slightly right and follow the red arrow. Ignore the next red arrow, on your right, and continue on the gravel path. Bear right at the Y junction (TQ 433 989), sticking to the gravel track, heading west. I advise you to take the OS Map to find this turning.

Follow the red gravel downhill, with ferns on either side of the path. Cross over the brook, or ditch if it's dry, and head up hill to the next car park. Cross the road to the metal gate. Continue following the gravel track to a steep downhill section, and bear right at the wooden fences. Head uphill on the red gravel, with the steep valley to the brook on your right. This is a particularly steep section of the walk. Ignore paths on the right and left and continue south. Ignore, too, the blue arrow.

This next turning is difficult to find. If you do miss it, you will emerge at the road slightly further up but that doesn't matter, you just have a bit more road walking to do. At grid reference TQ 418 969, about half way up the hill and by the no cycling or horse riding sign, turn left on the muddy path. This tree lined path takes you to the road. Turn left and follow Forest Road. Cross over at the main road and onto Station Road, following the signs to Loughton Station.

Owing to the wooded nature of this walk, it would be a very good idea to carry a map and compass. It is very easy to a take a wrong turn and end up in the wrong place! All trees look alike after a while. There are plenty of roads that intersect the forest, and you will more than likely stumble across one of these and you can use these to help get you back on track.

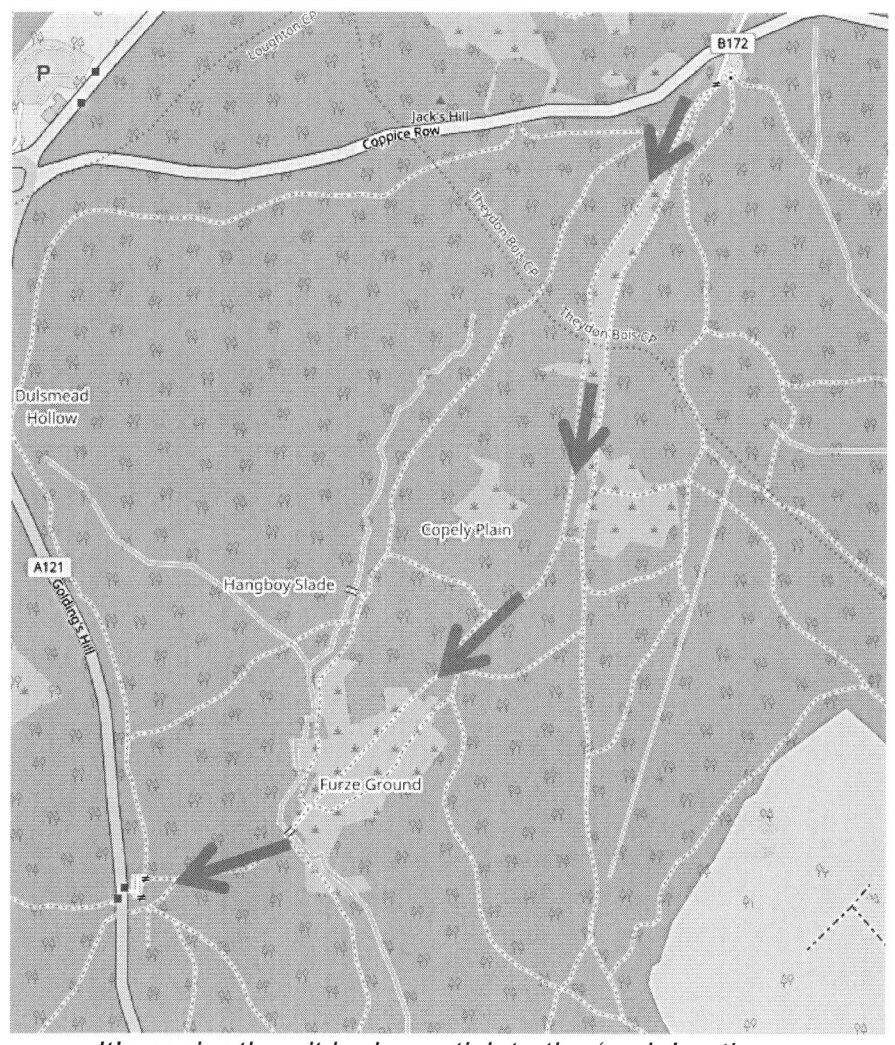

It's easier than it looks – stick to the 'main' paths.

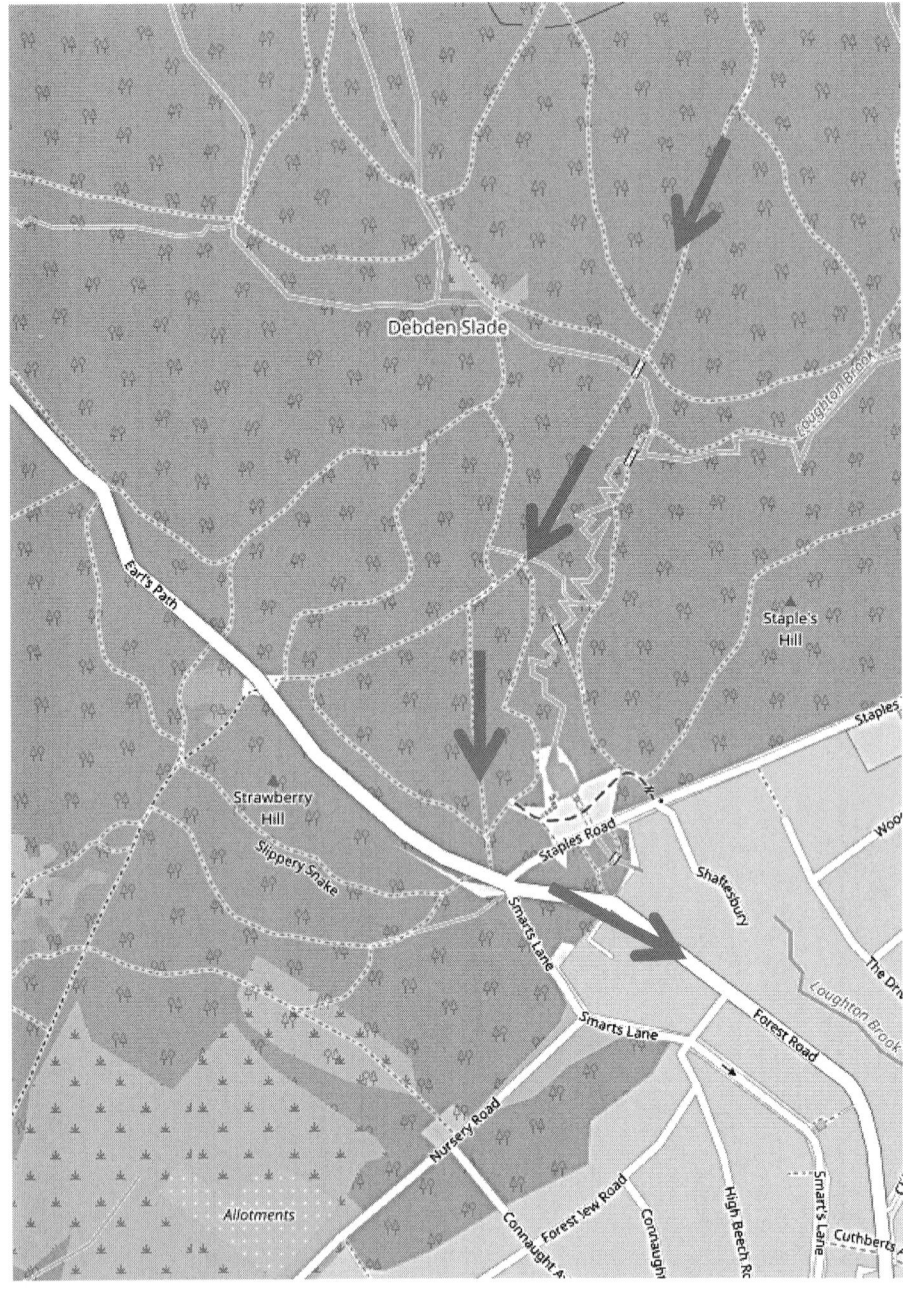

Morden to Putney Bridge

```
Morden              Northern Line           Zone 4

Putney Bridge       District Line           Zone 2

          Approx. 6½ miles    2½ hours

A wander down the quiet and peaceful River Wandle.
Mostly made tracks, but a few muddy sections.
```

    This enjoyable walk follows the River Wandle from Morden Hall Park to its mouth at the River Thames. The Wandle Trail, following the entire rivers route, begins in Croydon and is around 14 miles long in total. The trail is well signposted and uses a waterwheel symbol on signposts. Look out for these on local signs, cycle signs and way marking posts. Parts of the walk are on National Cycle Route 20. Look out, too, for blue plaques along the route showing how local people use the trail. Most of the route is on fairly well made paths; some sections may get a little muddy after some rain.

    The River Wandle was used heavily during the industrial revolution. Its water powered over 60 mills and you will visit a surviving mill on the walk. The river became one of the most polluted in England, effectively becoming a sewer. However, after much hard work, it has been cleaned. Now fish are returning and local fishermen report a variety of species to be found in the river. Look out for bird life too, made easier by the viewing platforms.

    Begin the walk at Morden Station, at the very southern end of the Northern Line. This section of the line can only be accessed from the Bank branch directly, if you're coming from the Charing Cross branch you will need to change at Kennington. Leave the 1920s station and turn left, following the main road. At the roundabout, turn left onto Morden Road. Use the crossing to enter Morden Hall Park.

Morden Hall Park, now owned by the National Trust, was originally owned by Westminster Abbey. In the grounds, water from the River Wandle drove a mill which ground tobacco into snuff. Now, there is a café and a garden centre in the grounds if you need a rest already! Turn left and follow the signs in the park if you want to visit these.

On entering Morden Hall Park, turn left and follow the gravel path, heading towards the blue sign posts. Pass the second blue sign post, and cross the tramway with care (remember to look both ways). Take the small wooden bridge and follow the signs for NCN 20. Keep right at the fork, following the gravel. The River Wandle is now on your right and on your left is Deen City Farm. Admission is free and you will reach the entrance shortly, a perfect trip for young animal lovers. At the road, bear right, going through the car park. Continue along the path, with the river on your right (see map).

Cross the road, using the bridge, and continue on the gravel path. Cross the next bridge on your right, and take some time to explore the Merton Abbey Mills. This used to be a textile mill, now there are places to eat and a craft market. William Morris, of printing fame, used the site and many of the buildings from his era still survive, including a water mill which still turns. There are also toilets on site. Leave the mill at the opposite end, crossing the bridge and re-joining the trail.

Cross the road and head through the brick arch. Bear right, crossing the smaller access road and find the fast flowing river. Take the tarmac path. Emerge at the main road, turning left onto Wandle Bank after the bus garage. Ignore the bridge on your right, and continue along the road. At the junction, go straight ahead onto the tarmac path and then immediately bear right onto the gravel path. Follow this along the river.

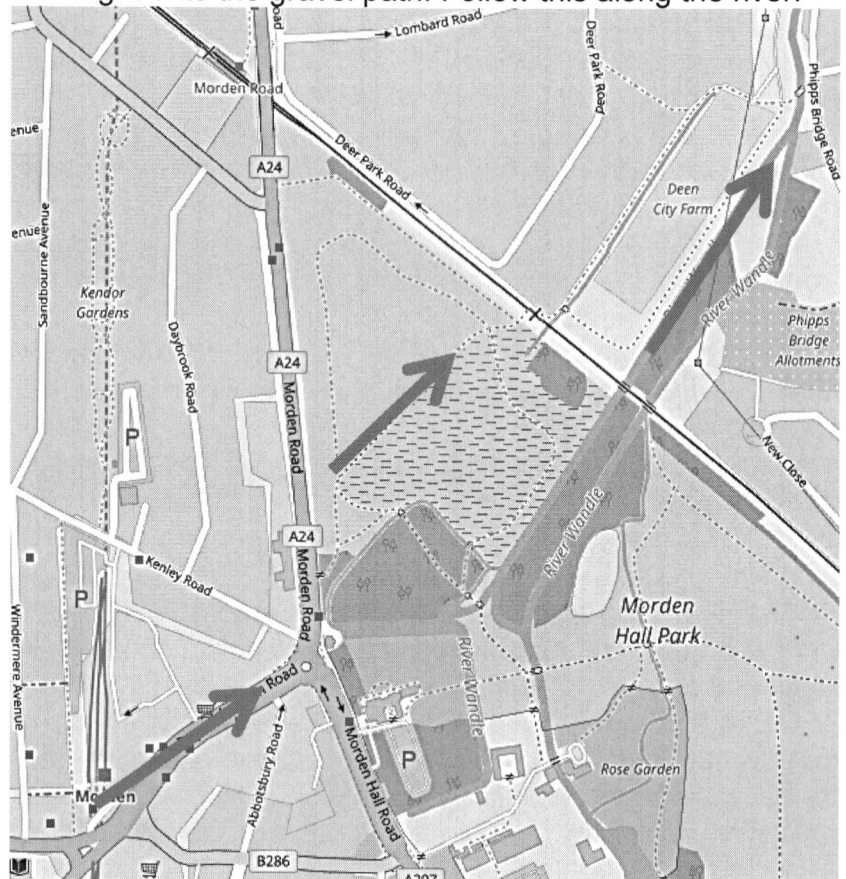

Cross the bridge on your right and head down the steps. Go straight ahead onto the gravel path. Follow this to the metal bridge, mind your head as you pass under! You are now in Wandle Meadow Nature Park, a local nature reserve. Follow the path north, in the direction of the power cables, but bearing slightly right, heading towards a kissing gate. Turn left onto the tarmac path, the river now on your left. Enjoy the view of the river from the metal viewing platform; it's a good place to spot the birdlife enjoying the river. (See map) Continue along the path. Cross the main road, turn left, then immediately turn right. Ignore the footpath on your left, keeping the river on your right.

At the next road, turn right and cross the bridge. Turn left onto Summerley Street. Turn left onto the main road, passing Earlsfield Station on your right. Turn left onto Penwith Road and then right onto Acuba Road. Enter King George's Park, sticking to the tarmac path, ignoring paths left and right. Follow the signs through the park, staying with the cycle path, following the river on your right. Cross the road and continue through the park. Bear right at the steep slope and when you reach the metal arch, follow the road. The river disappears for a while, and there is a section of road walking from this point.

At the main road, Garratt Lane, turn left. Follow this and cross Wandsworth High Street onto Ram Street. Turn left onto Armoury Way. Cross the bridge, and turn right onto The Causeway, the river reappears on your right. Continue under the railway bridge. Now you will see where the Wandle meets the Thames. Take the wooden walkway and reflect on the water you have been following as it passes London's historic landmarks and makes its way into the North Sea.

Head back and follow the Thames Path westbound, upstream. This is a well signposted national trail. Follow the Thames Path through Wandsworth Park, and continue with a short road section to Putney Bridge. Cross the bridge, beside the tube line and follow the signs to Putney Bridge Station. If walking in 'peak' times, you may be able to take advantage of the River Boat service (check the TfL website for details).

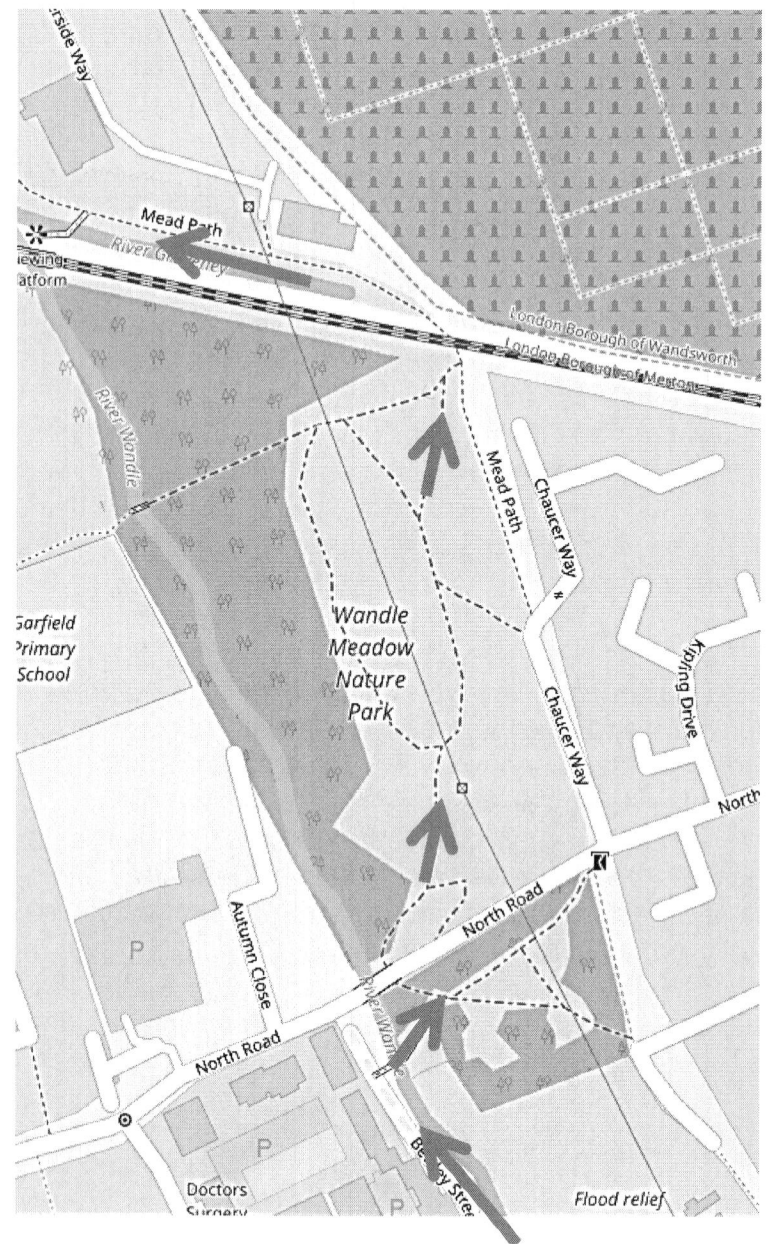

Cockfosters Circular

Cockfosters   Piccadilly Line   Zone 5

Approx. 4½ miles   1½ hours

Through historic woodland once used by Henry VIII. This walk can get quite muddy when wet, and there is a particularly slippery section too.

Trent Country Park has had many uses throughout its history. Many of the buildings, including the manor house, are grade 2 listed. Its last use was as a campus for Middlesex University, however this ended in 2012. Since then, there are controversial plans for housing on the site, as well as a museum in the house. The site dates back to the 14th Century, when Enfield Chase was a royal hunting ground, used by Henry 8th. One of the houses many owners included Philip Sassoon, who entertained the great and good, including Winston Churchill and Charlie Chaplin, amongst many others.

During the Second World War, Trent park was used as a Prisoner of War camp. Luftwaffe pilots and high ranking German Officers were brought to the park and kept in relative luxury, putting the prisoners at ease. Unbeknown to the prisoners, the rooms were bugged, allowing the British to find out all sorts of information! After the war, the estate began its long association with training teachers, first by the Ministry of Education, then Middlesex Polytechnic and finally Middlesex University. The park now boasts a wildlife hospital and animal sanctuary, a café and, for the adventurous type, a Go Ape centre. The park is famous locally for its daffodils in spring time and the field in front of the house is full of colour.

Exit the station through the car park and head through the metal gate opposite, following the London LOOP way marking. At the end of the cemetery, on your left, turn left through the copse. Leave the wooded section into an open field, ignoring paths to your right. Continue following the LOOP way markers into the next open field, bearing slightly right towards the driveway.

Cross the driveway, passing the white barrier, and continue into the car park, with the toilet block on your left. Take care as you cross the car park as it can be particularly busy, especially at weekends. Head towards the LOOP information board, behind the café and the ice cream stand. There is a children's play area on your left. Follow the LOOP through the woods, passing additional parking areas on your right. The path is well marked with LOOP way markers and round wooden posts with a single yellow band.

Head downhill, with open farmland on your left. Cross the small footbridge into the open field. Follow the gravel and dirt path along the bottom of the field. At the junction of paths, before the kissing gate and next wooded section, turn left. Continue following the path downhill, ignoring paths to the left, and follow the main path to the wooden sign post. As you walk, notice one of the two ornamental lakes on your right hand side. At the sign post, head uphill towards the 'Obelisk' (sign posted), leaving the LOOP at this point. The path up to the obelisk is reasonably steep, and can be very muddy and slippery when wet, thanks to the London Clay. As you head up, take a look behind you for your first glimpse of the main house.

Pause at the obelisk and take in the view over the park. The obelisk is inscribed:

TO THE MEMORY OF THE BIRTH OF GEORGE GREY EARL OF HAROLD SON OF HENRY AND SOPHIA DUKE & DUCHESS OF KENT 1702

The obelisk was brought to the park by Sir Phillip Sasson in 1934 when the then Duke and Duchess of Kent were honeymooning at the estate. The date is an error, as the child it refers to was born in 1732 and died soon after.

Turn right along the gravel path, heading east, through the woods. Bear right, following the main path, re-joining the London LOOP. Notice the kissing gate on your left, this leads to Camlet Moat. Very little is known about this site, although it is shown in local records as far back as 1440AD. It is said that the ghost of Geoffrey De Mandeville, once an earl but convicted of treason, haunts the site. When he was arrested, he hid his treasure in a well. Many have tried looking, but no one has been successful. Take some time to explore the site, before heading back to the kissing gate, turning left back onto the main path.

Head right at the LOOP waymark post, then left at the next post, walking towards the car park. Turn right at the sign post, following the sign for the bridleway (see map). Cross the car park driveway, following the path in the same direction. Cross the second driveway, then cross the bridleway. Stick to the main path, ignoring paths to the right, keeping in the same direction as the road, parallel, on your left. The path eventually bends right, heading south, away from the noisy road.

Pass through the kissing gates, crossing the bridleway. The path heads uphill. At the double bridge, continue uphill on the main path, ignoring the path and bridge on your left. Cross the next bridleway, again using the double kissing gates if the main gates are closed. Follow the sign post towards Cockfosters. The path soon becomes a tarmac and concrete driveway with cottages on your left. Ignore any left or right turns, sticking to the driveway. As you walk, you will pass the old university buildings on your right.

At the road, turn right*, following the road. As you round the bend, the main house will be on your right. If you've walked in spring, hopefully the daffodils will provide much needed colour. You can follow the loop round to the right, but sadly all the interesting and old buildings, the house, the sable yard and the orangery, are all fenced off at the time of writing. Pass the small obelisk, heading down another straight driveway. The animal hospital, with its café and play area, is on the left. Continue down the driveway to the Go Ape reception and the toilet block, this time on your right. At the driveway, retrace your steps back to the station, following the LOOP waymarks.

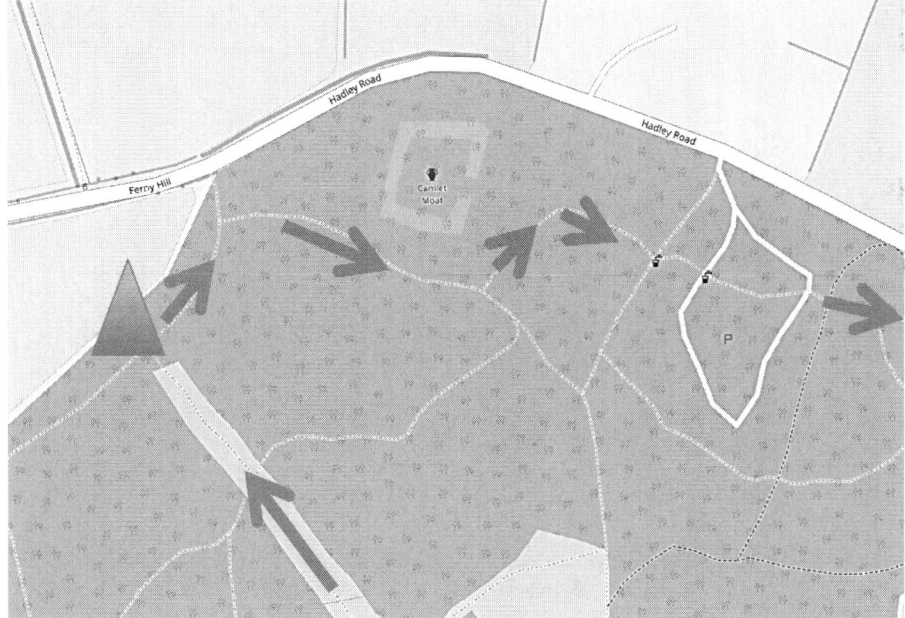

*You may want to extend this walk as it links nicely with the Oakwood to Arnos Grove walk. Instead of turning right to the main house, turn left and follow Snakes Lane to the main road. At the main road, cross onto Prince George Avenue to join the Oakwood walk to Arnos Grove.

Rickmansworth to Uxbridge

Rickmansworth	Metropolitan Line	Zone 7
Uxbridge	Metropolitan and Piccadilly Lines	Zone 6

Approx. 8 miles   3 hours

It's easy to forget how close you are to London on this rural towpath. Can be quite muddy, especially when wet.

The town of Rickmansworth, in southwest Hertfordshire, is in the 'Three Rivers' district council. The rivers Gade, Colne and Chess all meet near the town, all flowing into the enlarged River Colne, which meets the Thames at Stains. Water from these rivers feeds the Grand Union Canal, which we will be following on this walk.

One of the unique features of Rickmansworth is the 'frost hollow'. The town sits in a valley at the valley at the bottom of the Chiltern Hills and once cold air sinks into the valley it is trapped by the steep railway embankment. Because of this phenomena, the greatest ever temperature range recorded in England happened here when, in August 1936, the temperature rose from 1.1°C to 24.9°C.

Many mills relied upon the water flowing through the town, powering corn mills, silk presses, breweries, and paper makers. Rickmansworth Station is also served by Chiltern Railways and is on the London Marylebone to Aylesbury line. The station has three platforms, one for the Metropolitan line, one for the over ground and the third, now disused, is from the days of steam trains.

Like the other canal walks in this book, navigation is simple when we reach the canal. To get to the water, leave the station and turn right, crossing the road to the pedestrian subway. Turn left, and follow the noisy road, passing under the railway line and the fire station on your right. At Ebury roundabout cross the road, keeping the children's playground on your right. At the green arrow, marked 'Colne Valley Way', turn right and cross the bridge. You are now in the Rickmansworth Aquadrome Local Nature Reserve. The two lakes were formed during the construction of the first Wembley Stadium, when gravel was extracted from the area. The lakes are now used for recreational uses, as well as being an excellent local habitat.

After crossing the bridge, turn right, with the lake on your left and the toilet bock on your right. At the wooden sign post, turn left, following National Cycle Network route 61. Continue to follow the path to the reserve's café, the second lake now on your right. Turn left at the road, following signs to the 'canal centre'. At the road bridge, bear left and take the footpath to the canal towpath (see map).

Turn right onto the towpath. The first lock, Stockers Lock, and its keeper's cottage are grade 2 listed buildings and are nicely preserved. Shortly after you will notice a City of London coal post on your right. This marks the point at which coal being imported to London had to pay taxes. Ordinarily, this was not collected at the post, but when it reached its destination. However, there was a house built for the tax collector at this one so taxes were paid at this point.

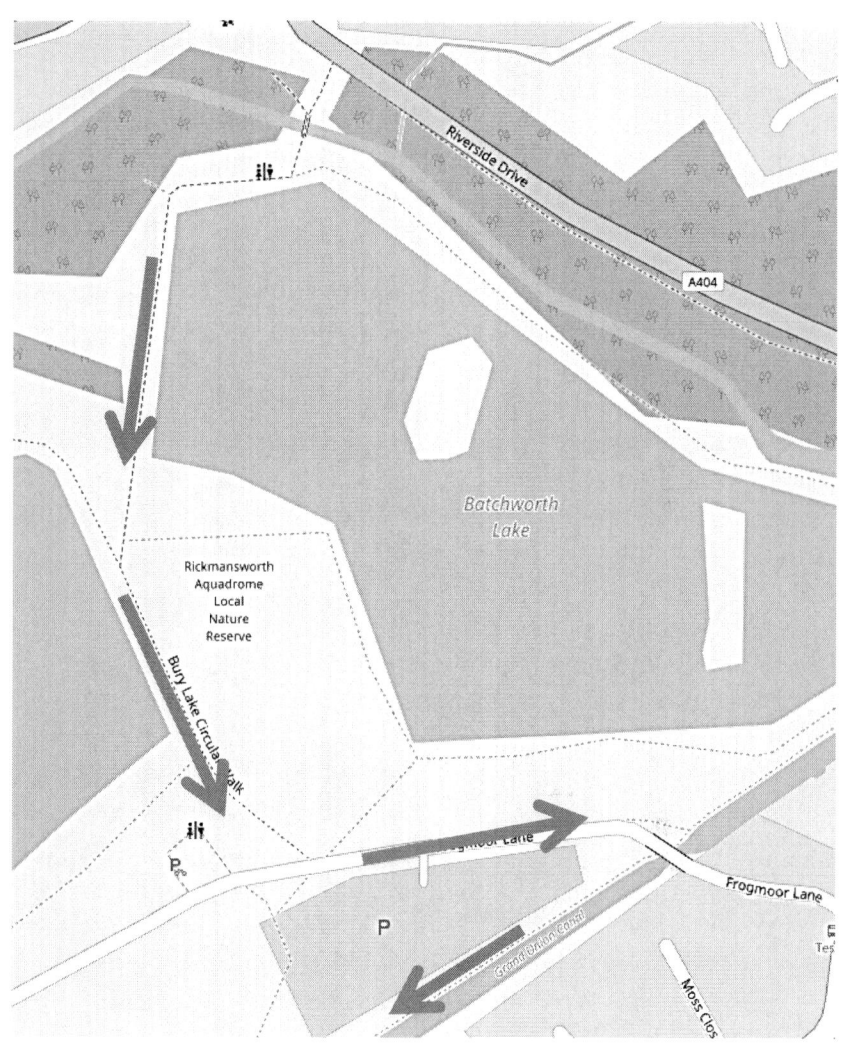

Continue along the towpath. The next stone marks the boundary between the Hertfordshire and the London borough of Hillingdon. As you pass the abandoned warehouse on your left see if you can spot it's guardian. Look out for the small black signs low down on the path. 'GJC C° Braunston 76 Miles'. The Grand Union Canal used to be called the Grand Junction Canal but changed its name in 1929 when several different canals merged to become one. At Braunston, the canal joins the Oxford canal. Continue to Springwell Lock, ignoring paths to your right.

Cross the bridge, ignoring the kissing gate on your right. You will soon be passing by Springwell Reedbed. The reedbed provides a vital cleaning service, improving the water quality for the River Colne and the canal. Cross the bridge over the boat works and see the sewage plant on your right. Continue along the towpath, passing the white cottage on your right and Hillingdon Narrow boat Association on your left. At Coppermill Lock, and pub, walk under the bridge.

At the next bridge, you will join the London LOOP, lookout for the waymarks on your right. Next you will see Black Jack's Mill on your right. Now a bed and breakfast, the mill can trace its origins to the Doomsday book of 1086. Legend says that the name derives from a serf who used to deliver flour using a donkey. He was so cruel to the donkey that children named him 'Black tempered Jack', and so the name stuck.

The next section of the walk feels very rural and it's hard to imagine that you are less than 15 miles from the centre of London. There are fewer moorings and so less human activity on this section of the canal. This means you are more likely to spot the many different types of bird using the canal. Pass under the old bridge, past Wide Water Lock, continuing along the towpath. Head under the railway bridge, continuing to Denham Lock. Take some time to enjoy a homemade cake from Fran's Tea Shop down the steps. Back on the towpath, ignore the footpath to the right and continue to the noisy dual carriageway. Use the bridge to cross to the opposite bank and pass under the A40. At Uxbridge Lock, cross the canal again. Pass the marina on your left. Leave the towpath at the Swan and Bottle Pub.

Climb the steps to the road and turn left to cross over the canal. Cross the road, following the signs to Uxbridge station. Keep Fountains Mill Young People's centre on your right as you cross the next road, climbing to the high street. As the road turns left, continue straight into the pedestrianized shopping precinct and to the station on your left.

Tottenham Hale to Stratford

Tottenham Hale	Victoria Line	Zone 3
Stratford	Circle, Jubilee Lines DLR & TFL Rail	Zone 2/3

Approx. 5 miles   1¾ hours

Between the towpaths of the Lee Navigation and the banks of the River Lea, taking in the marshes and surrounding woods. Can be muddy when wet.

This walk switches between the River Lea and the Lee Navigation. The beginning of the walk passes by the Lee Valley Reservoir chain, a group of 13 reservoirs that supply London with its vast demand for water. The Lee Navigation is a canalised river running from Hertford to the Thames, with the river beginning in the Chiltern Hills and ending at the Thames at Bow Creek. There is a lot of confusion over the names and spellings of the river and the canal. Typically, 'Lee' is used for manmade elements, such as the canal, and the 'Lea' used for the natural river. This confuses many people, including me, and so you may come across both spellings used at different points.

Leave Tottenham Hale station onto the pedestrianized concourse. Turn left, heading up the steps to Ferry Lane (A503). Turn left, crossing the railway. Cross Mill Mead Road then turn left onto the Lea Valley Walk. Head down the steep slope to Tottenham Lock, then turn right to head south along the towpath. Look out on the left for the river joining the canal.

Continue along the towpath, passing Markfield Park on your right. There are toilets and a café in the park if needed.

Continue along the path noticing the old cranes above you. As you turn south, notice the bank on your left. Behind this is the West Warwick Reservoir, holding 180000000 imperial gallons of water! Carry on walking south to the Lea Rowing Club. Head over the footbridge and leave the canal behind for a short while. Pass the marina fence and gates on your right, following the tarmac path as it bends to the right. At the gravel junction of paths, turn right to enter Walthamstow Marshes. From here, in 1909, the first All British aeroplane flew. The 90 acre SSSI is home to a variety of species, including the rare marsh warbler. Follow the gravel path, ignoring the paths to the left and the footbridge to the right. You may notice cattle on the marsh, replicating the ancient land management techniques. If you do come across the cattle, keep calm, give them space and don't panic if they follow you. Signs will give you more information.

Head under the railway bridge and continue to the cattle grid. Immediately after the cattle grid, turn left onto the grass path. Ignore footpaths left and right, and continue towards the high tension cables ahead of you. At the end of the field, turn right. At the black signpost, bear left onto the concrete path. Cross the footbridge and turn right, passing under the busy Lea Bridge Road. Follow the path as it bends left, then right. Ignore the footpath on the left, instead crossing over the footbridge and into Hackney Marshes (see map).

Originally a true marshland formed by the flooding of the River Lea, it was drained in the Medieval period. Later, rubble from bomb damaged buildings was dumped here during the Second World War. Now, particularly at weekends, the marshes are busy with local football teams playing on the many pitches. As you cross the river, at the junction of paths, turn left. Follow the River Lea through the peaceful wooded section. At the wooden bollards, turn right towards the car park. Pass the Hackney Marshes Centre and café on your right, heading towards the road.

Cross the road and walk down the slope into Wick Woodland. Head straight ahead, following the path as it bears slightly right, heading south. At the wide path, turn right, heading west. When you reach the black railings, turn left. At the information board, bear right to head under the busy dual carriageway. Emerge onto the towpath and turn left, following the canal on your right (see map).

At the dark red bridge, turn left, up steps to Copper Street. Go past the Copperbox Arena and turn right onto the main road. Cross the bridge over the River Lea heading towards the Westfield Centre. Construction and events, particularly West Ham home games, often close or restrict ways through to the station so lookout for signs. Be aware, also, that Stratford Station is different to Stratford International Station, although the DLR serves both. The ending of this walk can be noisy and full of traffic, but with the Olympic Park and the shopping experiences, to take your mind off the noise.

Westbourne Park to King's Cross

Westbourne Park	Circle and Hammersmith & City	Zone 3
King's Cross	Circle, Northern, Hammersmith & City, Piccadilly and Victoria	Zone 1

Approx. 5 miles   1½ hours

A variety of settings on this walk, from the extremely rural feel of Regent's Park to the noise of Camden Lock. All on a well-made towpath and some road.

The Regent's Canal provides a ribbon of peace through hectic North London. This is the second walk along this canal, this time west of the Islington Tunnel. See *Mile End to Angel* for a walk on the eastern side of the tunnel. The walk begins in a busy area of west London, before passing the more peaceful setting of Regent's Park. It then passes the hustle and bustle of Camden Lock before reaching King's Cross.

Leave the Westbourne Park station, turn left, following the road. Pass under the dual carriageway then turn left onto Elkstone Road. Enter the park and then turn right onto the towpath. Follow the towpath, passing the Canal and River Trust's building on the right. Walk under the low bridge to Little Venice.

Little Venice is the point at which the Grand Union Canal, which we've been following to this point, becomes the Regent's Canal. The 'Lagoon', or Browning's Pool, has a café and river bus services, operating in peak season. After you've explored the pool, head over the bridge and continue along the canal walking north east. The other branch continues a short distance to Paddington. Follow the Regent's Canal on your right until you reach the private moorings.

When you can go no further along the towpath, head up the slope to Blomfield Road. Turn right, walking in the same direction as the towpath. At the Maida Hill tunnel, cross the road onto Aberdeen Place. The 272 yard tunnel opened in 1816 with spoil from the digging being used to level land which subsequently became Lord's Cricket Ground. As you walk along Aberdeen Place, notice the blue plaque on the left, showing where Guy Gibson, of Dam Busters fame, once lived. Ignore roads left and right and as the road bends left, take the alleyway beside the electricity substation. Follow the path high above the canal to the main road, Lisson Grove. Turn right, to cross Frampton Street, then cross Lisson Grove, turning left. Take the second, smaller, gate on your right to head down the steep slope re-joining the canal towpath.

Follow the path, with the canal on your right. Pass the moorings and the gardens, perhaps dreaming of living on narrow boat. Pass under the bridges and notice the impressive houses and gardens on your right. These villas include the residence of the American ambassador. Next you will come across a bridge with green pillars. This is known as 'Blow Up Bridge', because a boat carrying gunpowder exploded here. In the early hours of the morning, on 2nd October 1874, as the boat exploded, locals leapt from their beds fearing an earthquake. The explosion caused three deaths and the bridge collapsed. When it was rebuilt, the pillars were turned, giving the towropes a smooth surface. You can see the grooves cut by the ropes.

As you pass through Regent's Park notice how quiet it has become. You will soon be among the animal exhibits of London Zoo, noticeably the aviary on your left. At the end of the park, the canal turns left. Continue along the towpath to the busy Camden Lock. Fight your way through the crowds, keeping the canal on your right, ignoring the footbridge to the right. Pass Hawley Lock and then Kentish Town Lock, minding your head under the low bridges.

Pass the old gas works on the left. They are now being converted to apartments; I wonder what the Victorians would make of that! Pass St. Pancras lock then lookout for the steps up to Granary Square. Cross the bridge over the canal, crossing the road, and head down King's Boulevard to the station entrance on your right.

Nearby is the London Canal Museum. If you want to find out about the history of the canals or see inside a narrow boat, it is a great place. It is located in Battlebridge Basin, on the south side of the canal. The museum is closed on Mondays (open bank holidays), and is open all year round. Check their website for details: www.canalmuseum.org.uk.

Richmond to Southfields

Richmond	District Line	Zone 4
Southfields	District Line	Zone 3
	Approx. 7 miles	2½ hours

Explore this London park, famous for its deer population. An historic royal hunting ground, now popular with walkers. Mostly on grass and dirt paths with some road walking.

Richmond Park is designated as a SSSI, a national nature reserve and special area of conservation. It is the second largest park within London, coming second to the Lea Valley Park, which we explored in an earlier walk (*Tottenham Hale to Stratford*). It was created in the 17th Century to be a Royal Deer Park and they can still be found within the park.

There are around 30 ponds that support a variety of wildlife, including woodpeckers, snakes and a flock of parakeets, who reportedly escaped from captivity to become a breeding flock in the park. The park is generally open throughout the day, although there can be restrictions in February and November when deer culling can affect access. The park also has bridleways and cycle routes, so be aware as you walk through the park.

Leave the station and turn right onto the main road. At the police station, turn right onto Church Road. At the junction, cross to stay on Church Road, climbing to the large church at the top of the hill. Bear left, then right, onto Friars Stile Road. Pass through the local shops to Landsdowne Gate, one of the entrances to Terrace Gardens. The gardens, overlooking the River Thames, were formed from three different 18th Century estates. They opened in 1887 as a public park. Now, after much investment, there are a wide variety of plants, better signage and a café. Enjoy the view down to the Thames, before turning left to follow the slope down through the park. Pass the statute of Aphrodite on the way down. Keep to the slope, ignoring the steps, passing the Hollyhock Café on your left and the glasshouse on your right. Have a peek inside and see what exotic plants are growing. Continue to the road.

Cross the road and turn left to follow the Capital Ring. Keep to the concrete path, passing through Pelham Meadows. Be aware that at certain times of the year cattle graze the meadow. Go through the kissing gate with the riding centre on your left. Follow the path to the church, turning left alongside the graveyard, still following the Capital Ring.

Emerge from the path at another road. Cross the road to enter Richmond Park at Petersham Gate. There is a toilet block and a children's playground on your right. Follow the signs for the Capital Ring uphill on a wide grass path. Look out for the way marking posts bearing right at the top of the hill. From the top of the hill you can see the control tower of Heathrow and the distinctive National Archives building.

Continue following the Capital Ring waymarks, passing Pembroke House on your left. This Georgian Mansion was home to a secret reconnaissance unit during WW2. The path climbs steps to a road. Cross the road and continue on the tarmac path. At the gravel junction of paths, bear left, following the Capital Ring. Pass through the wooded section to Richmond Royal Oak tree, a tree said to be from the 1200s. As you leave the woods behind, leave the Ring temporarily, keeping straight ahead on a smaller grass path (see map). Keep your eyes peeled for the deer that roam this part of the park.

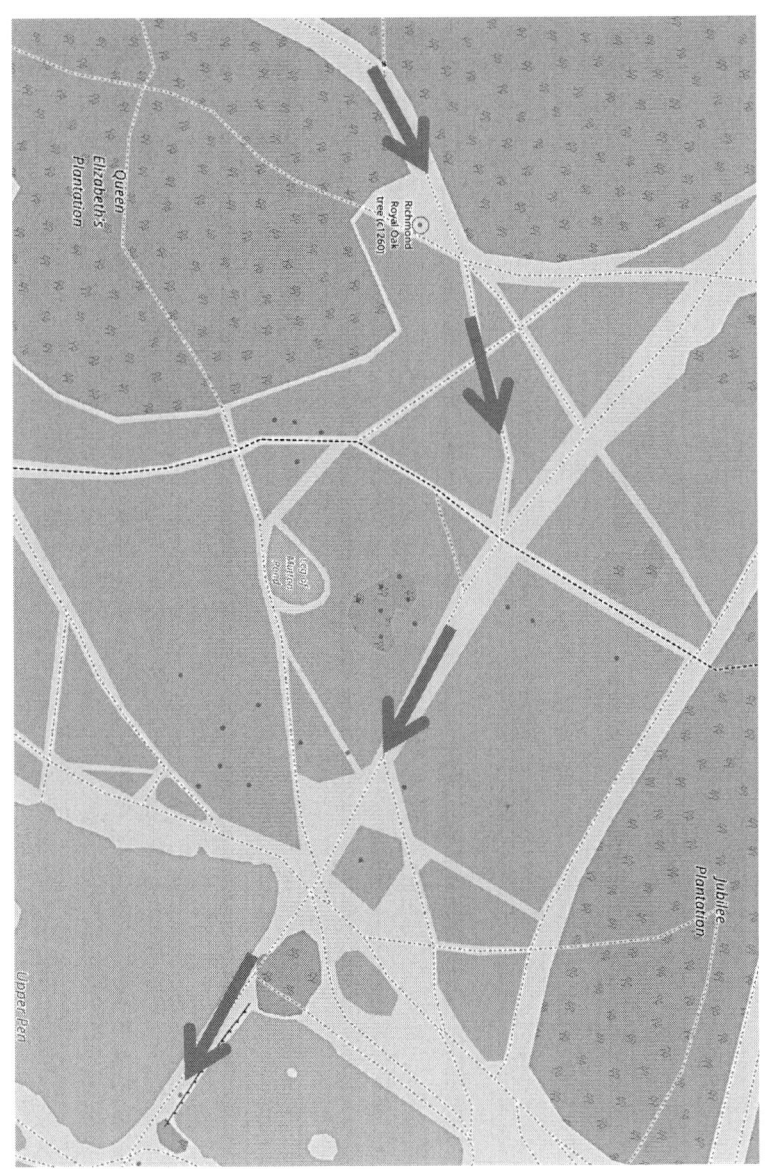

Re-join the ring at the main path, turning right towards the two large ponds. Walk between the two, continuing straight ahead on the gravel path. Notice the White Lodge on your left, a former royal home, now it houses the Royal Ballet. Pass the car park, with the café, on your right, keeping in the same direction on a grass path. As the path bears left, following the perimeter of the woods, keep straight ahead. The Capital Ring has lost its arrow from its waymark post. Cross the road by the small car park and bear right to the black gates.
    Cross the main road and enter Wimbledon Common. This is one of the largest areas of heathland in London. Make sure you keep your eyes peeled from the famous Wombles! The common is a SSSI and is home to a number of unique plants. Bear left after the Pegasus crossing (a crossing for horses too), then bear left at the junction to cross the footbridge. Turn right, going through the wooded section, with playing fields on your left.
    At the footbridge over the brook on your right, bear left, climbing on the bridleway through the woods. Continue climbing, ignoring paths left and right and pass a horse exercise area on your right. Keep to the sandy path, bearing left and heading north east, as you pass through the golf course. On the right, you pass a memorial stone to the King's Royal Rifle Corps, marking the fact that the troops trained here during the WW1. Keep east on the path until you reach the wide path where you turn left, walking north (see maps).

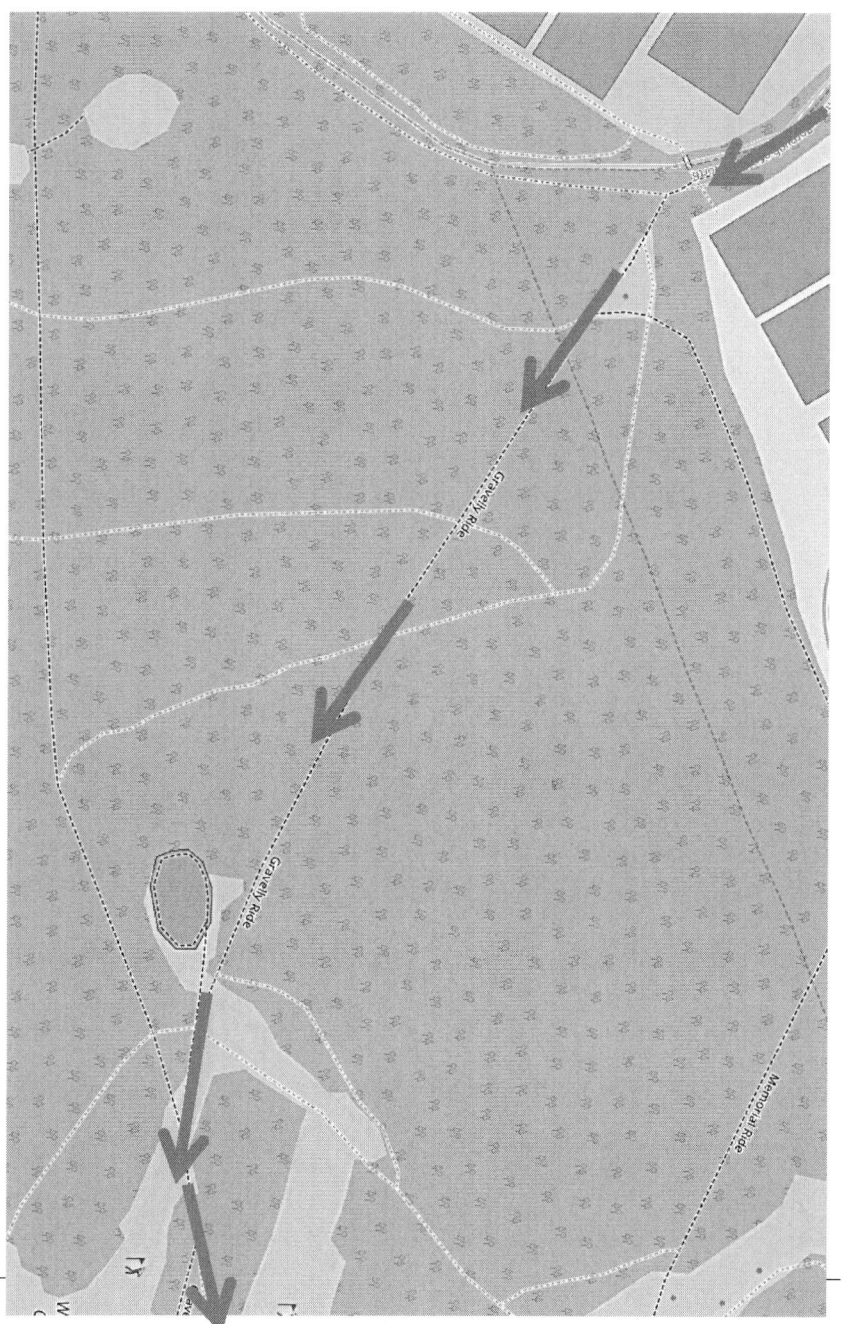

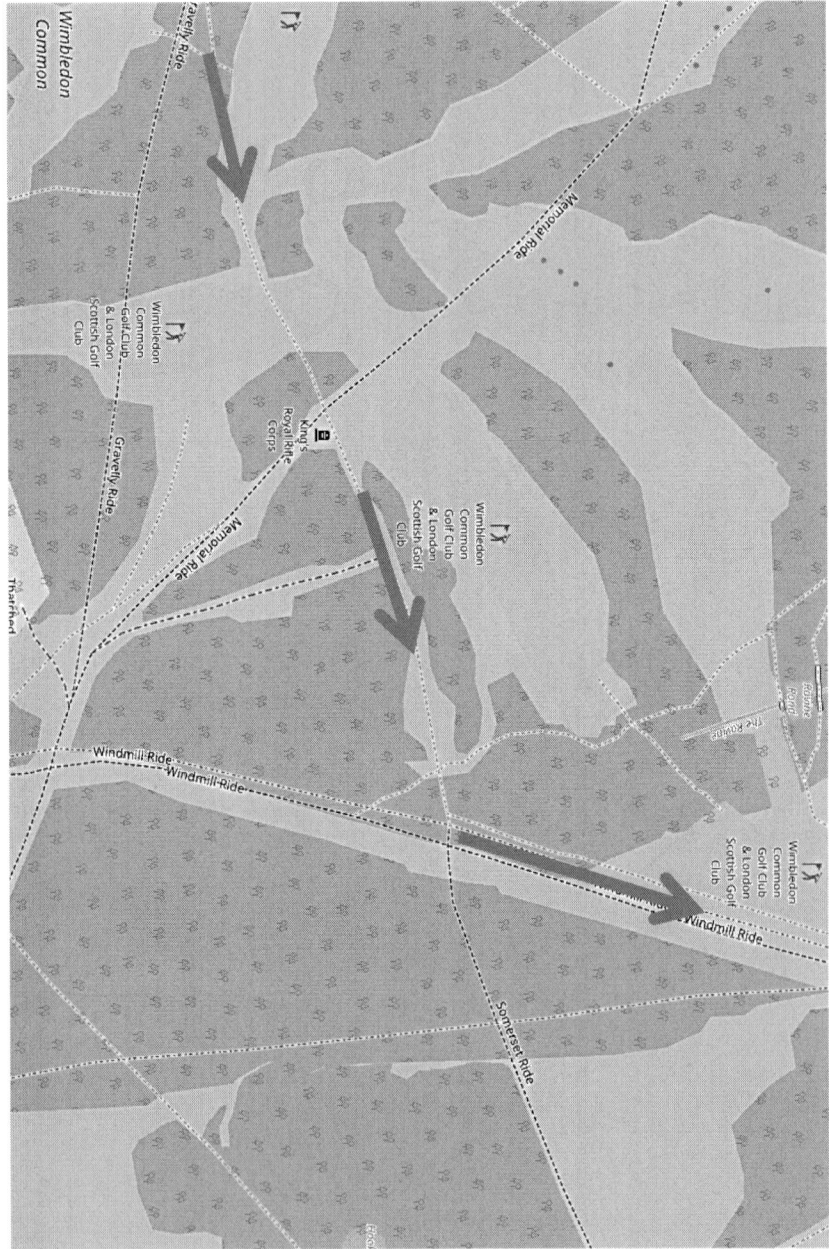

Soon you reach the windmill, a grade 2 listed building. This is where Baden-Powell wrote part of his 'Scouting for Boys'. There is a museum, which is open during peak season only, see www.wimbledonwindmill.org.uk for more details. Turn right, to follow the road to the white gate. Immediately before the gate, turn left to pass behind the buildings on a public footpath. Turn right, to keep the buildings on your right, then cross the road. Turn right onto Queensmere Road, rejoining the Capital Ring. Turn left onto Bathgate Road, then left on Wimbledon Park Road. Ignore the Ring sign pointing right through the park, but continue on the road to Southfields station.

Oakwood to Arnos Grove

Oakwood	Piccadilly Line	Zone 5
Arnos Grove	Piccadilly Line	Zone 4

Approx. 3½ miles   1 hour

A magnificent little stroll through North London's parks and open spaces. Mostly on tarmac paths, with a short wooded section including a steep climb. Some suburban road walking.

Thanks to Sue Davey (Twitter: @FisherLady21) for suggesting this route.

Oakwood likes in the southern end of Enfield Chase, a former royal hunting ground, believed to be used by Princess Elizabeth in the 1500s. Oakwood is named after Oak Lodge, which stood in Oakwood Park until the early 20th Century. The park was bought by the council in 1927 to be used as a public park.

Cockfosters Station is a wonderful art deco building and is Grade 2 listed. Like many of the Underground Stations at this end of the line, it was designed by architect Charles Holden. One of his ideas was to replace the box like structure of stations with a circular drum style, which you will notice as you reach Arnos Grove Station.

Leave the station and turn right. Pass by the small row of shops and cafes, and turn right into Prince George Avenue. At the large 1930s church, St Thomas's, bear left to stay on

Prince George's Avenue. As the road turns left, cross the road to enter Oakwood Park.

Follow the path and at the junction, by the park's information board, turn left. Continue along the avenue of trees on the tarmac path, heading east, then south, as the path turns right. The path turns right again, to head west. At this point, you need to ignore the gates and the road on your right. Turn left at the next fork, towards the electricity substation, and then emerge onto Oakwood Park Road.

Turn left to The Vale, then turn right. After Elmbank, turn left following the public footpath between two houses. At the road, turn left then turn right onto Park Gate. Cross Park View, to enter Grovelands Park. Originally a private estate, it is now a grade 2* listed building and on English Heritage's 'at risk' register. The house was built for Walker Grey, a Quaker brewer. The grounds include a lake, which when drained once, was found to be home to several terrapin turtles. The house is now part of the Priory Hospital and is where General Pinochet was kept under house arrest in 1998, while a patient at the hospital.

Enter the park and turn left. Following the path down towards the woods, keeping the tennis and basketball courts on your right. At the footbridge, cross the brook then turn right, keeping the brook on your right. Head through the woods, passing the children's play area. Take the steep path up to the boating lake. If you don't like steep paths, you can keep to the tarmac, keeping the woods on your left.

Turn right with the lake on your left. At the crossroads, turn left on the tarmac path, keeping the lake on your left. At the end of the lake, bear right, with the pitch and putt course on your left. Follow the path to the road.

Turn left onto The Bourne, and then cross the road to The Greenway. Ignore roads left and right until you reach Norman Way. Bear right, then head along the public footpath beside the garage.

Cross the road using the zebra crossing, then bear left on the tarmac path to Arnos Grove (see map). Follow the road, ignoring all turnings left and right until you reach the roundabout at the bottom of the hill. Walk through the roundabout to the impressive gates at the entrance to Arnos Park, once part of the Arnos Grove estate. Bear left, following the tarmac path through the park. At the cross roads of paths shortly after, keep straight ahead. Cross the Pymmes Brook, a tributary of the River Lee, using the green, metal bridge. Climb Arnos Road and turn right on the main road to reach Arnos Grove Station. Notice Holden's round design at the grade 2 listed station.

Highgate to Finsbury Park

Highgate	Northern Line	Zone 3
Finsbury Park	Piccadilly and Victoria Lines	Zone 2

Approx. 3½ miles   1½ hours

A walk through the ancient woodland and nature reserves along a disused railway line to the popular and busy Finsbury Park. On woodland and gravel tracks.

The ancient woodland in North London is mentioned in the Doomsday Book, but there is even evidence of more ancient use. Prehistoric flint tools have been found, as well as an enclosure, probably for deer, dating back to the medieval period. There is also evidence of Roman use within the woods. Now it is owned and managed by the City of London Corporation.

Leave the station, using exit 3 to the main road. Turn right along Archway Road, then right onto Muswell Hill road. Cross the road to enter the woods, keeping straight ahead on the paths, towards the toilets and playground. Pass the children's play area on your left and continue to the open field ahead. Bear right, across the pitch, towards the café building. On the right is the excellent nature hut, giving details of the wildlife found within the woods, and plus a rather scary-looking stuffed fox!

Walk behind the café building, on a tarmac path heading north. Ignore the sign to the 'Store Yard', but continue to the green Capital Ring sign post. At the fountain, turn left, following the Ring on a dirt path. When you reach the entrance gate to the woods, turn right, leaving the Capital Ring at this point. Pass one of the keeper's cottages on your left, turn right, heading uphill. Cross the tarmac path, keeping in the same direction. Ignore the first gate on your left by the keeper's cottage; instead head past the red way marking post, to the second gate.

Leave Highgate Wood, crossing the road to the Queen's Wood Local Nature Reserve, opposite. Historically, this was all part of the same woodland that covered a huge amount of North London, Hertfordshire and Essex. Now the woods are home to a large amount of bird species, including wood peckers. Listen out for them as you walk.

This section includes some steep hill sections. If this is an issue for you, see the notice at the entrance to Queen's Wood. Head downhill towards the café. Bear right, following the Capital Ring Waymarks. Head downhill, and at the crossroads, keep straight on following the Capital Ring. The gravel path then climbs steeply, before becoming steps. Bear right at the junction, heading towards the road. Bear right at the junction, towards the quiet road. Cross the road to continue in the woods, following the Capital Ring. Steps make the descent a little easier. Cross the brick bridge and climb on the steep tarmac path to the road.

Turn right and follow the road. Look out for the public footpath between houses on your left. Turn right to the main road and then turn left. Turn left onto Holmesdale Road and walk downhill. Enter the Parkland Walk through a gate on your left. This is a former railway line that connected Finsbury Park and Highgate. It closed in 1964, despite pre-war plans for use by London Underground. After its closure, it was designated a nature reserve in 1990 and now has many information boards to give you details about the flora and fauna to be found.

Turn right and follow the track bed. Ignore any access paths left and right as you pass between houses. You will reach the old Crouch End Station, where only the platforms remain. Continue along the track bed, passing over and under bridges until you reach the black gates that mark the entrance to Finsbury Park.

The park was one of the first London Parks to be built during the Victorian era. It now boasts sporting and leisure facilities as well as hosting many events. Cross the bridge over the railway. Turn right at the tarmac path, following the Capital Ring sign to Finsbury Park station. Bear right at the small children's play area, following the tarmac path to emerge at the road with the station ahead of you. You may want to explore Finsbury Park at the end of this walk, and you may find that Manor House station at the northern end of the park is more convenient.

Woolwich Arsenal Circular

> Woolwich Arsenal   DLR   Zone 4
>
> Approx. 9 miles   3½ hours
>
> A long circular walk, taking in the Green Chain walk, a ruined abbey and the Thames Path. There are some densely wooded section on this walk, and also some walking through housing estates – very diverse!

Woolwich Arsenal is named because the site used to belong to the Royal Arsenal, which carried out explosives research and manufacture for the military. The Board of Ordinance bought the former house in the 17th Century and the site grew massively in the lead up to WW1. The site closed as an ordinance factory in 1967 and the Ministry of Defecnce moved out in 1994. Now the site is being extensively redeveloped into housing. Firepower – the Royal Artillery Museum and the Greenwich Heritage Centre all explain the areas past in greater detail.

Leave the station and turn left to Vincent Road. Turn right onto Burrage Street, climbing to Trinity Methodist Church. Turn left onto Plumstead Common Road, then left onto St. Margaret's Grove. Turn right onto the concrete path, following the sign for the Green Chain Walk. This is a walk that is around 50 miles, see www.greenchain.com for further details. At the crossroads of paths, continue in the same direction. Pass the memorial to the 8th London Howitzer

Brigade on your left and then bear left past the adventure playground.

Continue to the road, cross to the path in the same direction. Ignore steps to the right, keeping to the chain walk, passing tennis courts on your left. Cross the road, keeping in the same direction. At the meeting of paths, turn right to the road, then turn left on the path parallel to the road. Cross the smaller road, Warwick Terrace, following the path. Before the path heads downhill to the crossing, turn left. At the green signpost, turn right, taking care as you descend the steps to Slade Pond on your right. Bear left, ignoring the steps to your right, but climb steps to the road.

Cross the road to Winns Common. Turn left to the path that runs parallel to the road. Cross the tarmac path, keeping to the Green Chain Walk. Bear right with the path, passing the basketball court on your right. The path descends, before climbing again, with small woods on your left. Do not enter the woods, but continue to the road. Cross the road, heading straight across the field, aiming for the green signpost, keeping the small mound on your right. At the dead tree by the signpost, descend using the steps into Great Bartletts Woods. Keep descending, following the way marking posts. Emerge from the woods onto a path between houses and then to a road.

Cross the road to Rutherglen Road, then walk down the steps on your left, following the sign to 'Bostall Woods'. The path bends right, passing behind the houses. Bear left, climbing through the woods, continuing to follow the Green Chain Walk waymarks. The woodland gets thick, but the excellent waymarks easily point the way through the woods. Ignore the smaller paths to your left and right, continuing west through the woods. Emerge from the woodland, to pass the bowls club on your left (see map).

Cross the road, following the way marking posts. Keep the woods on your right, to reach the next road. Cross the road, turn right, then left at the signpost to 'Bostall Heath'. Keep to the path, crossing the access track, ignoring the sign and leaving the chain walk temporarily. Continue along the path to the road, crossing carefully to Hurst Lane. Ignore the first kissing gate on your left, entering the woods by the second kissing gate. These are Lesnes Abbey Woods, ancient woods that can trance their heritage back to the Bronze Age.

Follow the waymarks to the pond on your right. At the pond, bear right, following the edge of the pond, then turn left, northwest, continuing along the path to the road. Cross the road to the kissing gate, ignoring the path to the left, keeping to the Green Chain Walk. Turn left at the waymark, to the Abbey Ruins.

Lesnes Abbey, now a scheduled ancient monument, was founded by Richard de Luci, the Chief Justiciar in 1178. The Chief Justiciar was effectively the prime minister of the day, being the King's chief minister. The abbey was closed in 1525 by Cardinal Wolsey, following the dissolution of the monasteries the previous year. The stone was sold to build other buildings in the local area. Explore the ruins and the gardens, before heading north across the long footbridge over the road and railway.

Now follow the Abbey Way stones, along a gravel path with children's play areas on your left. Keep north along this path until you reach the fishing lake. Bear left and emerge from the path at the road. Turn left, following the road, towards the flyover, where you will find steps up to a footbridge. Descend from the bridge using the slope then follow the line of garages along Byron Close, continuing in a northerly direction. Walk through the underpass, then turn left before the shops, keeping the brook on your left. Ignore the footbridge on your left, pass the school and continue to the road. Turn right and then use the crossing to safely cross the dual carriageway.

Turn right then turn left onto Linton Mead. Pass the gates, and keep straight ahead, descending steps to the Thames Path. Turn left, and walk alongside the industrial Thames, passing the containers and the factories that inhabit this end of the river. At the flooded and littered pill box, the path climbs to the cycle path. Where the cycle path turns left, keep to the Thames Path walking route, which is clearly signed. Continue to the old arsenal buildings and warehouses.

Lots of development and building works sometimes close the path and change routes, so you may need to refer to local signage. You will come across canons and sculptures of iron men by the river bus jetty. Turn left, passing the Firepower museum to the main road. Cross the road and enter the shopping precinct continuing to the station.

Further Walking

If you've enjoyed walking these routes, there are plenty of other walks throughout London. Look in your local bookshop or library and you are bound to find lots of walking guide books for London, taking you into the city or exploring certain aspects, such as murders or graveyards.

For further walking, you may like to try the London LOOP. The London Outer Orbital Path, sometimes described as the M25 for walkers, is 150 miles long and is clearly signed throughout its route. It sticks to outer London and tends to head through fields, woods and parks. The Capital Ring is shorter, being only 75 miles, and passes through more urban areas of the city. Guide books are available for both the Capital Ring and the London LOOP and the routes are marked on OS Maps too.

If you want to explore even further, you may want to try the Thames Path. The entire path runs from source to sea, and is over 180 miles long. Again, guide books exist for this walk and are often split into the rural section and the London section.

Other routes also exist and a quick search on a local authority website may produce some excellent walking routes for you to plan your own days out. If you don't want to plan your route, you could join one of the many walking groups the capital can offer. Again, a quick search online will provide you with all the details.

Note

All the walks in this book were correct at the time of writing. If you find that walks and routes have changed, please let me know for future editions. Get in touch, too, if you spot any inaccuracies in the background research of the location featured.

Along with this book, it is always advisable to carry an OS map or an A-Z style map in case of difficulties. OS Explorers 161 (London South), 162 (Greenwich & Gravesend), 173 (London North) and 174 (Epping Forest & Lee Valley) cover the walks used in this book. OS Landrangers 176 (West London) and 177 (East London) could also be used, but don't carry the detail that might be required when walking.

Always be prepared for the walk and the weather and carry suitable supplies for your adventures. Pack enough food and drink to keep you going, and always let someone know where you are going.

If you have any walks that you feel could be included in a future edition of this book, again please contact me.

Happy walking,

Nick

nicktaylor1989@live.com   *Twitter: @_flash_writer*

#0234 - 211116 - C0 - 210/148/4 - PB - DID1658365